MY JOURNEY
TO THE STARS

To my daughters,
Samantha and Charlotte

Picture credits: Key: t—top, b—bottom, c—center, l—left, r—right
Dr. Jorge Cartes and Tim Gagnan: 2; Mark Kelly: 37 (r); Scott Kelly: 4, 8 (bl), 14; NASA: 1, 6, 8
(br), 27, 32, 33 (t, b), 35, 36, 37 (l), 38, 40 (t, c), 44, 47 (t); NASA/Bill Ingalls: 47 (c, b), back cover;
NASA/Scott Kelly: 40 (b), 45 (t, b); NASA/Tim Peake: 43; NASA/Stephanie Stoll: 4; Star-Ledger
Photographs © The Star-Ledger, Newark, NJ: 20, 21; Jerry P. Tarnoff: 23; US Navy/VF-143—The
World Famous Pukin' Dogs: 30–31.

Visit us on the Web!
rhcbooks.com

Educators and librarians, for a variety of teaching tools, visit us at RHTeachersLibrarians.com

Library of Congress Cataloging-in-Publication Data is available upon request.
ISBN 978-0-525-64861-1 (trade) | ISBN 978-1-5247-6378-7 (lib. bdg.) |
ISBN 978-1-5247-6380-0 (pbk.)

Printed in the United States of America
10 9 8 7 6 5 4 3 2 1

MY JOURNEY TO THE STARS

by Astronaut Scott Kelly
with Emily Easton
illustrated by André Ceolin

Crown Books for Young Readers  New York

4

It has been 340 days
since I set foot on Earth.
I have spent almost a full year
living and working on
the International Space Station,
or the ISS.
I miss fresh air.
I miss hugging my daughters
and girlfriend, Amiko.
At last,
it is time to get
into the spaceship
that will take me home.

I climb into my seat.

The spaceship is very small.

My two Russian crewmates sit so close

to me, our elbows touch.

We all strap ourselves in.

It is going to be a wild ride!

My twin brother, Mark,
is waiting for me back
on Earth.
We are the only brothers
in NASA history to fly in space.
We were born on
February 21, 1964,
in Orange, New Jersey.
Mark was born six minutes
before me.
We have spent our lives
like partners in crime.

We grew up in West Orange
surrounded by family.
It felt so safe that Mom sent
Mark and me across the street
to mail a letter
when we were just five.
We walked to the corner to cross.
We mailed the letter.

But on the way home,

Mark didn't want to follow

Mom's rules.

I walked to the corner.

Mark crossed in the middle

of the street.

I heard car brakes screech.

My brother got hit!

SCREEEEEECH!

Mark was rushed to the hospital.
I had to stay with our uncle
and eat liver for dinner.
Mark came home with a great story.
I felt like I got the worse deal.

Mark and I took a lot of risks.

Sometimes we both got hurt.

But each time,

we aimed higher.

This was great training

for the biggest risk of all—

becoming astronauts.

Every weekend,
Mark and I stayed
with our grandparents
so Mom and Dad could go out.
Every week, Grandma and Pop Pop
took us out to breakfast.

And every week,
we visited amazing gardens.
Years later, I remembered those
garden visits as I took care of
the flowers on the ISS.

At home,

every day was different.

Our parents didn't always

get along.

It was scary when they argued.

Mark and I would hide in our room.

Watching our parents fight turned

Mark and me into peacemakers.

This has helped us each lead

our own crews in space.

You never know when your problems

can become your strengths.

Dad was a police officer.
When I was eleven years old,
Mom decided to become
a police officer, too.

In the 1970s, women could
finally join the police force.
But first they had to pass
the same test that men did.
My father set up a training course
in our backyard.
I was Mom's practice dummy.

19

The hardest part of the course
was the wall Mom had to climb.
At first, she could not even
touch the top.
It took a long time,
but Mom finally did it.

She passed the test
and was one of the first
female cops in New Jersey!
She showed us that if we had a plan,
with small steps we could turn
a big dream into something real.

A REAL-LIFE
POLICE STORY

I didn't know what my dream was.

I was a terrible student.

I could not sit still.

I could not listen to the teacher.

I could not stop watching

the squirrels out the window.

But Mr. Tarnoff, my principal,

believed in me.

He begged me not to give up.

Years later, he was my guest

at both of my space shuttle launches.

During high school,
Mark and I joined
the volunteer ambulance unit.
Every night was different.
We liked helping people.
I had finally found
something I loved.
I would become a doctor.
But how was I going to get
through college
and medical school?

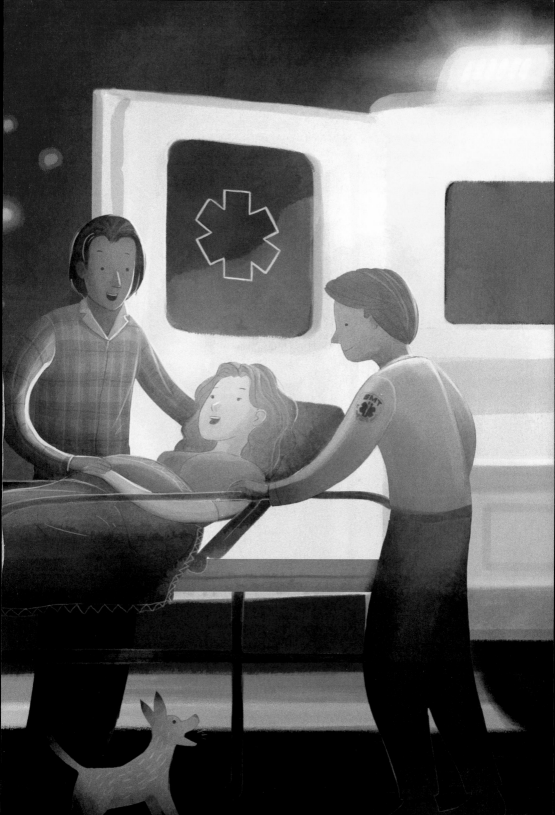

One day, a book
called *The Right Stuff*
caught my eye.
It changed my life forever.
Daring pilots risked it all.

How fast could they go?

How high could they fly?

Sometimes pilots crashed.

Sometimes they soared.

The best became the first

NASA astronauts.

I finally found my dream!

I wanted to be a test pilot.

And thanks to Mom,

I knew how to make my dream real.

I would make my plan.

I would follow it step by step.

Step one was doing my homework.

Now that I had a goal,

I worked hard and graduated.

Step two was joining the navy.

Now I could learn how to fly.

Mark started flight school, too.

I took a lot of risks flying jets.

I needed to see how fast

my plane could fly.

I needed to see how good a pilot

I could be.

Flying a fighter jet was hard.

The first time I tried to land on

a moving ship, I couldn't do it.

But I didn't give up.
In the end, I flew faster
than the speed of sound.
Then I wanted to fly
higher and higher.
To do that, I needed to
go to space.

Mark and I joined NASA in 1996.

MARK   SCOTT

SCOTT

MARK

We each flew into space four times.

We flew on a space shuttle

and on the ISS.

But we never went to space together

in case something went wrong.

Space travel was our biggest risk of all.

I flew the space shuttle *Discovery*

on a mission to fix

the Hubble Space Telescope.

And I led the space shuttle

Endeavour on a short mission

to make the ISS bigger.

The space shuttle stopped flying in 2011.

Now the only way to reach the ISS

is on the Russian Soyuz.

Then NASA asked me to spend

a year in space, which would

set an American record.

NASA hopes to send astronauts
to Mars one day.
First, they need to see what happens
when humans are in space
for a long time.

MARS

Twin astronauts were perfect
for this job.
One twin in space tested
his blood, eyes, muscles, and bones.
One twin on Earth tested the same.
NASA will keep studying our body
changes now and in the future.

MARK
ON
EARTH

SCOTT
IN
SPACE

On the ISS,

there is no gravity,

so you float around.

Sometimes your body can float away

when you are sleeping.

That's why the crew has to sleep

in bags that hang on the wall or ceiling,

drink through a special straw,

and use a special bathroom

that is like a vacuum cleaner.

My crew on the ISS was so busy.

NASA told us when to eat, exercise,

and work in the lab.

We ran 400 experiments.

We even grew plants in space.

I liked to water the flowers.

It reminded me of seeing gardens

with Grandma and Pop Pop.

I liked eating the lettuce even more.

We were the first crew to eat food

grown on the ISS.

NASA did its best to keep us safe.
But the ISS is always at risk.
Our crew faced extra dangers
during my year in space.
We lost two unmanned ships
bringing fresh food and supplies.

The space station was almost hit
and destroyed by space junk.
And we had to make an emergency
space walk to fix the ISS.

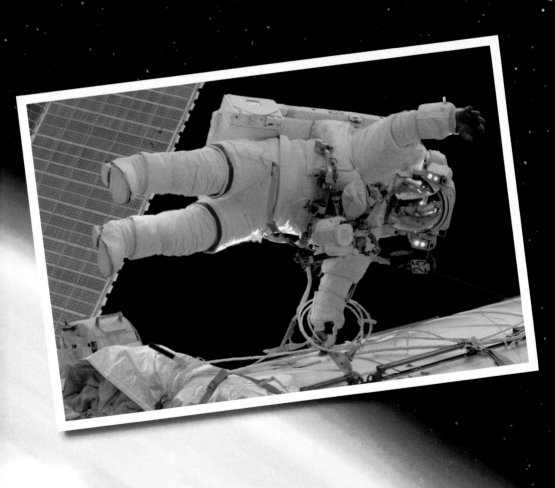

We missed Earth so much
and loved to look out the windows
at our beautiful planet.
We saw cities shining at night.
We saw rivers and oceans
in many shades of blue.
We wanted to share the beauty
and inspire people to help
protect our amazing home.

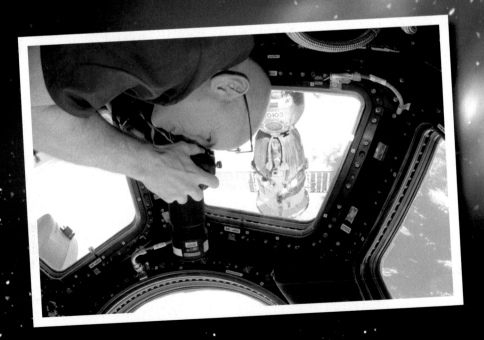

HOUSTON

NEW ORLEANS

THE BAHAMAS

Finally, my mission is done.

It feels good to know that the risks

I've taken bring humans closer to Mars.

Now it is time to go home.

Our Soyuz capsule is falling back

to Earth at almost

one thousand feet per second.

Gravity presses down on us.

The parachute opens.

The landing is hard.

My head slams into the seat cushion.

Then the hatch opens.

47

The fresh air smells amazing.

I hug my family.

I get poked and prodded by NASA.

At last, I return to Texas.

I jump right into my pool fully clothed.

The sights, smells, and sounds
of Earth surround me.

It feels so good to be home.